CONTENTS

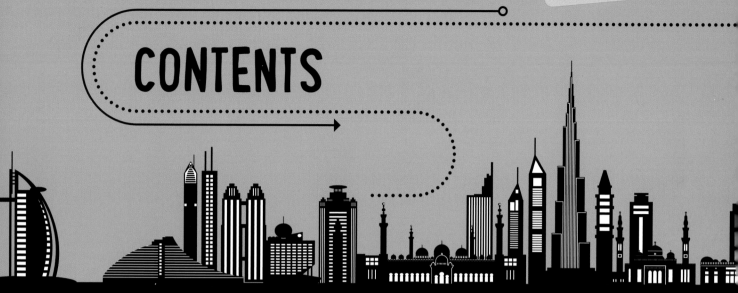

STARTING OUT

BUILT STRUCTURES ARE ALL AROUND US, FROM EVERYDAY HOUSES AND OFFICES TO HUGE SKYSCRAPERS AND MEGA BRIDGES. CREATING ANY BUILDING, WHETHER BIG OR SMALL, REQUIRES A LOT OF HARD WORK AND CAREFUL THOUGHT.

The architects of the Lloyd's Building in London wanted to create a spacious, open-plan working space. They designed the building with pipes, lifts and electricity cables on the outside to create more space inside.

When people decide to construct a new building, they have to go through a planning process. There are lots of important questions to be answered at every stage.

STEP 1

CONCEPT What is the purpose of the building? How big does it need to be? What features does it need?

STEP 2

DESIGN How will the building fulfil the aims set out in the concept? What will it look like? Will it stay up and be safe to live and work in?

STEP 3

CREATION How can the design be converted into a real building? How much of each material is needed? How long will it take to build?

PROJECT

- Choose a building in your neighbourhood and think about its concept. Describe its purpose, features and size.

- Why do you think its creators chose this concept?

- Do you think they were successful?

- What could be changed to make the building more useful or attractive?

BUILDINGS

ADVENTURES IN
STEAM

Izzi Howell

WAYLAND
...oks.co.uk

Published in paperback in Great Britain in 2019 by Wayland

Series editor: Izzi Howell
Designer: Rocket Design (East Anglia) Ltd
Illustrations: Rocket Design (East Anglia) Ltd and Julian Baker
In-house editor: Julia Bird/Catherine Brereton

ISBN: 978 1 5263 0458 2
10 9 8 7 6 5 4 3 2 1

FSC
MIX
Paper from
responsible sources
FSC® C104740

Wayland
An imprint of
Hachette Children's Group
Part of Hodder & Stoughton
Carmelite House
50 Victoria Embankment
London EC4Y 0DZ

An Hachette UK Company
www.hachette.co.uk
www.hachettechildrens.co.uk

Printed in Dubai

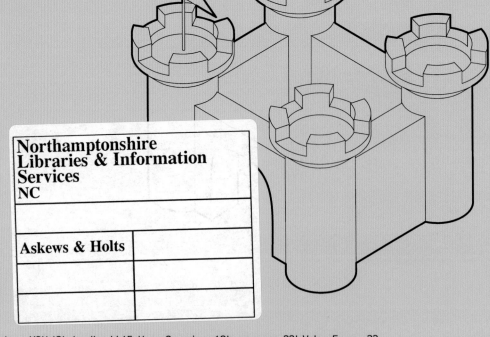

Picture acknowledgements:
Alamy: Historic Collection 42; iStock: pa_YON 12b, kpalimski 15, HomoCosmicos 18b, rmnunes 23l, ValeryEgorov 23r, Ismailciydem 24tr, erlucho 25t, Agenturfotograf 26b, nidwlw 27, pics-xl 28, hippostudio 33tr, david franklin 35br, espiegle 39t, oversnap 39bl, Leonid Andronov 41, Julian Baker: 30b and 43; Shutterstock: alice-photo cover and title page, Ray_of_Light 3 and 12-13t, Dan Breckwoldt 4 and 24bl, voyata 7, Guzel Studio 8, vagabond54 10, Alfredo Cerra 11, KWSPhotography 16, Renata Sedmakova 17, Vorobiev Aleksey 19, kornilov007 20t, mircea dobre 20b, Kotsovolos Panagiotis 21t, Rvector 22, vvoe 24tl, Atomazul 25bl, Elnur 25br, Terry Kettlewell 26t, Olena Mykhaylova 29, stockelements 30t, Igorsky 31, majeczka 32t, Natali Glado 32bl, Artur Bogacki 32br, joreks 33tl, Capricorn Studio 33b, pashamba 34t, poo 34c, Ariyaphol Jiwalak 34b, Sander van der Werf 35t, MISHELLA 35br, Paul Broadbent 36, iulianmarcu 38tl, HelloRF Zcool 39tr, Travel Stock 38b, leungchopan 39br, thelefty 40, Rahhal 44, chombosan 45.

All design elements from Shutterstock.

The website addresses (URLs) included in this book were
valid at the time of going to press. However, it is possible that
contents or addresses may have changed since the publication
of this book. No responsibility for any such changes can be
accepted by either the author or the publisher.

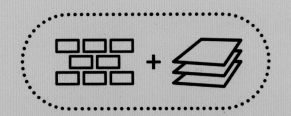

IT TAKES A CREW OF PEOPLE WITH DIFFERENT SKILLS TO DESIGN AND MAKE A BUILDING.

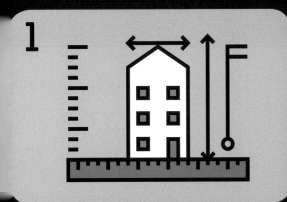

1

Architects use their creative skills to design and draw plans for the building. City planners check that the building will be a useful addition to the community.

2

The architects work closely with structural engineers, who use their knowledge of physics to make sure that the weight of the building will be properly supported and that the building will be able to resist forces, such as wind.

3

Building services engineers plan systems for heating, cooling and lighting the building.

4

Finally, builders use their practical skills to construct the building.

TECHNOLOGY TALK

Today, architects and engineers can use computer programs to plan and test buildings before they are constructed, preventing potential mistakes! In the past, architects and engineers could only rely on their knowledge and experience when designing a building, which makes ancient structures even more impressive.

MATERIALS

THERE ARE MANY THINGS TO CONSIDER WHEN CHOOSING A MATERIAL FOR A BUILDING. ARCHITECTS MAY PREFER CERTAIN MATERIALS FOR THEIR VISUAL APPEAL AND COST. THEY ALSO NEED TO THINK ABOUT WHETHER THEY WILL WORK WITH THEIR BUILDING'S DESIGN. ENGINEERS CONSIDER A MATERIAL'S STRENGTH AND SAFETY.

The first buildings were made from naturally occurring materials, such as wood, mud and stone. Later, humans learned how to produce and manipulate concrete, bricks, glass and metal. Today, we tend to use a combination of different materials in every building, with heavy bricks and concrete for the structural elements and glass for the windows.

SCIENCE TALK

Pure metals, such as iron, don't usually make good building materials. This is because they are easy to bend, as their atoms are all the same size and can easily slide past each other. Alloys, such as steel, have atoms of different sizes. It is much harder for the structure of their atoms to change shape, so they make much stronger building materials.

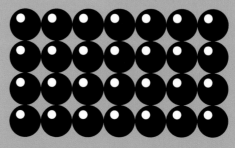

The atoms in iron are all the same size.

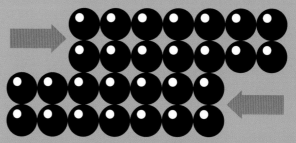

Iron will distort easily as the atoms slide past each other.

THINKING OUTSIDE THE BOX!

Sometimes, traditional materials can be reinvented for modern designs. Instead of using large blocks of stone to construct walls, the Japanese architect Kengo Kuma sometimes uses thin slices of stone to decorate the outside of his buildings.

In his design for the Asakusa Culture and Tourism Center in Japan, Kengo Kuma spaced thin slices of wood along the windows in different ways to offer more or less privacy to the rooms inside.

Today, scientists are developing smart materials, which can change in response to temperature, pressure or moisture. One of the most incredible smart materials is self-healing concrete. When cracks appear in the concrete, it exposes tiny pods of bacteria and calcium to the air and rain. These substances react with the rainwater to create more concrete, which seals the cracks!

Graphene is a promising material made from carbon atoms arranged in hexagons. It is incredibly thin, yet hugely strong – around 200 times stronger than steel! Scientists believe that covering buildings with a mixture of graphene and paint could protect them against weather damage.

" ART TALK

The appearance of materials is also important when designing a new building. Architects often choose colours and textures that complement or contrast with each other. For example, rough, red bricks will stand out against smooth, grey metal.

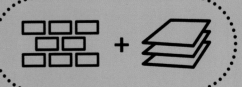

STRUCTURE

MAKING A BUILDING STAY UP REQUIRES CLEVER ENGINEERING, AS UNBALANCED FORCES ACTING ON A STRUCTURE CAN BRING IT CRASHING TO THE GROUND.

Gravity can be a serious risk to construction if it isn't managed properly. The force of a building's mass being pulled towards the Earth by gravity is known as its weight. If the weight of a building pushes down harder than the Earth's surface can resist upwards, the building will sink into the ground. This is why it is important to construct buildings on solid, dry ground.

The famous Leaning Tower of Pisa in Italy was built on soft, unstable ground. It started leaning during construction in the 12th century.

ENGINEERING TALK

Underground foundations stop buildings from being tipped over by turning forces. When a force, such as the wind, puts pressure on the side of a building, the foundations resist and push back in the opposite direction. This balances the forces and stops the building from falling over.

HOW GRAVITY MAKES A WALL COLLAPSE

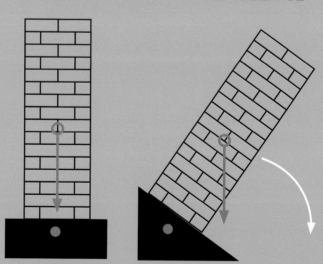

Gravity can also make buildings fall to one side. If a building's centre of gravity is not above the centre of its base, gravity will create a turning force called a moment. This force will push the building over.

Metal or wood beams are often built inside walls and floors to help structures withstand forces. An unsupported ceiling can only bear a small amount of weight from the floor above without caving in. Adding horizontal beams in the floor that run across to the walls means any weight placed on the ceiling is transferred sideways and supported by the stronger vertical walls.

THINKING OUTSIDE THE BOX!

Rectangles are not particularly strong shapes for building as they easily change shape or collapse if you push on their sides. If you add a diagonal beam across a rectangle, you create two triangle shapes. This makes the rectangular wall much stronger, as you cannot distort a triangle without breaking its beams.

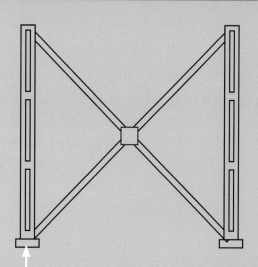

Adding two diagonal beams will make a rectangular wall even stronger, as it is divided into four triangles instead of two.

ENGINEERING TALK

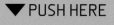
▼ PUSH HERE   DISTORTS

 =

If you push on the side of a rectangle, it can change into a parallelogram without breaking its sides.

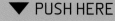
▼ PUSH HERE   NO CHANGE

 =

If you push on the side of a triangle, it will only change shape if you exert enough force to break its sides.

PROJECT

- Make a triangle and a rectangle from Blu-tack and toothpicks. Use a blob of Blu-tack at each of the corners.

- How easy is it to distort the rectangle into a parallelogram?

- What happens if you add a diagonal toothpick across the rectangle?

- Are isosceles and right-angled triangles as strong as equilateral triangles?

ARCHES AND DOMES

ALTHOUGH ARCHES AND DOMES LOOK FRAGILE, THEY CAN SUPPORT GREAT WEIGHT. THE SECRET TO A STRONG ARCH IS COMPRESSION – A SQUEEZING FORCE THAT SUPPORTS THE CURVE WITHOUT ANYTHING UNDERNEATH IT!

Roman architects (see pages 20-21) were obsessed by arches and used them everywhere, from bridges and aqueducts to giant public buildings, such as the Colosseum in Rome, Italy. As arches have an empty space in the centre, they can be stacked to make tall walls that weigh much less than standard structures.

The Roman aqueduct in Segovia, Spain, is still standing today. There is no mortar sticking the stones together – the pieces hold each other in place.

KEYSTONE

SCIENCE TALK

Instead of pushing straight down, the weight of an arch is pushed outwards from the keystone (central stone) along the curve to the supports at each side. These supports push back, creating a compression force that keeps the arch from collapsing. However, this force is only created when the arch is complete, so arches need to be supported by a frame while they are being constructed.

PROJECT

- Build an arch from ice cubes.

- How could you stick the ice cubes together?

- How could you support the rest of the arch while you are adding new pieces?

- How could you change the shape of the ice cubes to make them fit together better?

THINKING OUTSIDE THE BOX!

If you rotate lots of arches around a central point, it creates a half-sphere shape, also known as a dome. Domes make dramatic ceilings or roofs and are often used in religious buildings. Like an arch, the weight of a dome is transferred outwards to the edge of the curve. It is supported by the walls underneath, which push back, balancing the force.

OCULUS

The domed roof of the Pantheon in Rome has an oculus (hole) which provides natural light. The centres of the stone blocks that make up the domed room have been carved out to reduce weight and for decoration.

Modern geodesic domes are made from triangle-shaped pieces rather than a circle of arches. Each triangle is made from glass or plastic, held in place by a metal frame. The metal structure distributes weight across the entire dome, which means that it does not need strong walls underneath for support.

DESIGNING A BUILDING

DESIGNING A BUILDING MAY SEEM LIKE A PURELY CREATIVE TASK WITH NO LIMITS, OTHER THAN THOSE OF YOUR IMAGINATION! HOWEVER, WHAT LOOKS EFFORTLESS IS ACTUALLY A CAREFUL COMBINATION OF MATHEMATICAL RULES TO MAKE BUILDINGS LOOK BALANCED AND ATTRACTIVE TO THE EYE.

If you look closely at a building, you'll see that it is made up of a combination of 2D and 3D shapes. Rectangular doors and square windows are easy to spot. The main body of a building may be a cuboid or a cube. Pyramids, cones and spheres may be used to add interest at the very top.

" MATHS TALK

Many buildings have a vertical line of symmetry. This means that if you draw a vertical line down the centre of the building, the shape of the building and the windows and doors on either side are the same. Symmetrical buildings look classical and elegant, while asymmetrical buildings tend to look more modern and unusual.

The symmetry of the Grand Palace in Bangkok makes it look dignified and stylish.

Dubai is home to some of the most architecturally interesting large buildings and skyscrapers in the world. Which 2D and 3D shapes can you see in the buildings that make up its skyline?

As well as choosing strong materials that will support the building, architects also consider materials based on their visual appeal. Materials can be combined and positioned in different ways to create patterns to decorate the outside of buildings.

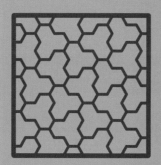

MATHS TALK

Many building materials, such as bricks and tiles, have regular shapes that can tessellate. This means that they can fit together in a repeating pattern without gaps and without overlapping. You can see these patterns on the outside of buildings. Squares, rectangles, hexagons and triangles all tessellate by themselves. You can also combine shapes, such as octagons and squares, to create more elaborate patterns.

PROJECT

- Design your own tessellating pattern. Use two shapes, such as triangles and squares.

- How many different patterns can you create using the same two shapes?

- Which materials could you use to add your pattern to the side of a building?

- How could you make a tessellating pattern using circles?

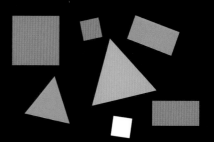

SCALE AND PLANS

ONCE YOU HAVE THE IDEA FOR A BUILDING, YOU NEED TO DRAW YOUR PLANS SO THAT YOU CAN SHARE THEM WITH OTHER PEOPLE. ARCHITECTS PLAN THE INSIDE AND OUTSIDE OF A BUILDING – NOTHING IS LEFT TO CHANCE!

It would be ridiculous to draw a life-size design for a building. Instead, architects draw smaller plans using scale. Scale drawings give an accurate idea of how the final result will look. Inside plans are usually drawn in more detail than outside plans, as architects need to check if they have left enough space for rooms and furniture.

MATHS TALK

In scale drawings, all measurements are reduced by the same amount. For example, a scale of 1:200 means that 1 cm on the page is 200 cm in real life. 1 m on the page would be 200 m in real life. What is the scale shown in this image?

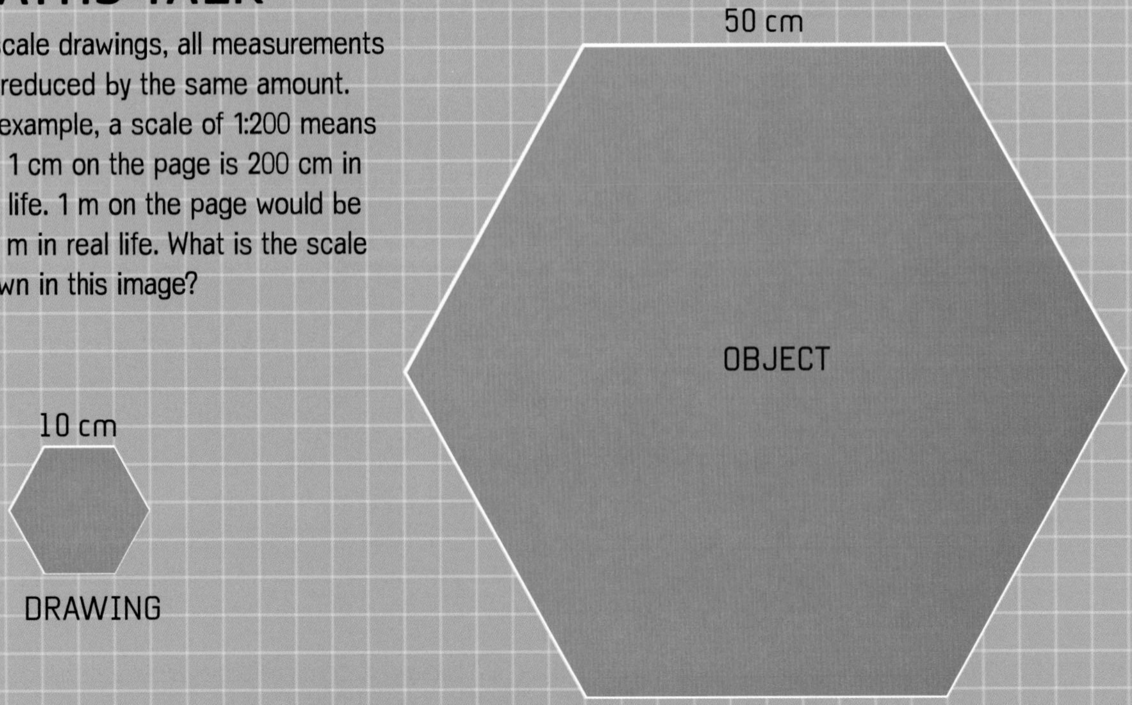

50 cm

OBJECT

10 cm

DRAWING

Architects do different types of drawing to show each part of a building. The inside of a building is often drawn as a floor plan. This is a flat aerial view, with doors, windows, stairs and furniture marked in place. Architects will design a plan for each floor in a building.

These plans show two floors in a family house. How are the stairs, doors and windows marked on the plan?

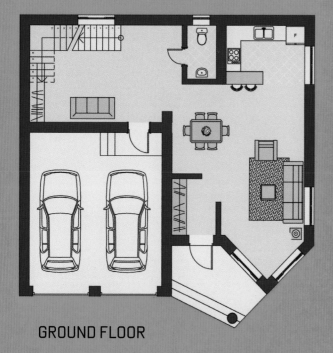

GROUND FLOOR

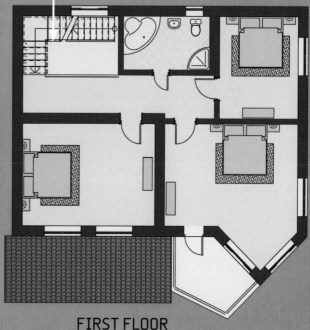

FIRST FLOOR

PROJECT

- Draw a floor plan of your bedroom. Measure the walls and furniture with a tape measure and choose a scale that fits the page.

- Which scale will you use? How will you mark windows and doors?

- How detailed can you make your drawing with the scale you have chosen?

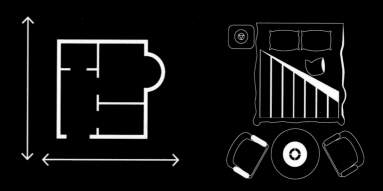

PERSPECTIVE

FLAT FLOOR PLANS ARE VERY USEFUL, BUT SOMETIMES WE NEED A CLEARER IMAGE OF HOW A BUILDING WILL LOOK IN REAL LIFE. DRAWING IN PERSPECTIVE ALLOWS US TO CREATE A 3D VIEW OF A STRUCTURE ON A 2D PIECE OF PAPER.

The general idea of perspective is to make objects appear on the page as they do in real life. To do this, nearby objects need to be drawn larger than faraway objects.

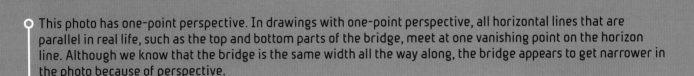

This photo has one-point perspective. In drawings with one-point perspective, all horizontal lines that are parallel in real life, such as the top and bottom parts of the bridge, meet at one vanishing point on the horizon line. Although we know that the bridge is the same width all the way along, the bridge appears to get narrower in the photo because of perspective.

VANISHING POINT

HORIZON

PARALLEL IN REAL LIFE

THINKING OUTSIDE THE BOX!

Painters have not always used perspective as we do today. They drew items to be taller or shorter depending on their importance, rather than their distance from the viewer. However, in the 15th and 16th centuries, people started trying to use maths and science to understand the world. Taking a mathematical approach to art helped them to understand perspective and apply it successfully to their artwork.

Leonardo da Vinci's mural of The Last Supper, completed in the late 15th century, has one-point perspective. Jesus's head is located at the vanishing point to make him stand out from the others.

Some architectural drawings use two-point perspective. This is a style of perspective in which horizontal lines can meet at one of two vanishing points along the horizon line. All vertical lines stay parallel and never meet. If you are drawing a very tall building, you may need to use three-point perspective, in which one vanishing point is above or below the horizon.

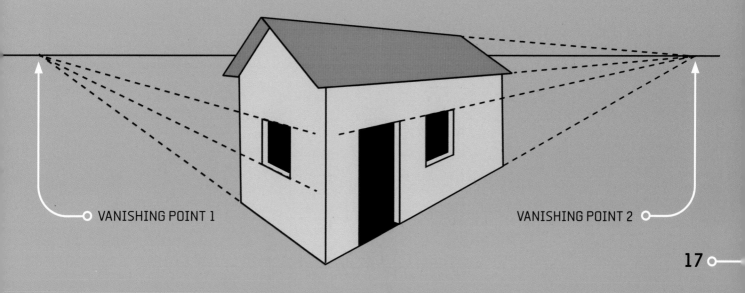

VANISHING POINT 1

VANISHING POINT 2

ANCIENT BUILDINGS

THE FIRST HUMAN-BUILT STRUCTURES WERE PROBABLY MADE FROM WOOD, MUD AND ANIMAL SKINS. THESE BUILDINGS HAVE SINCE DECOMPOSED, BUT SOME STONE BUILDINGS FROM ANCIENT CIVILISATIONS STILL REMAIN, GIVING US A FASCINATING INSIGHT INTO EARLY ENGINEERING AND TECHNOLOGY.

Ancient builders built structures for some of the same reasons as we do today. Most ordinary people lived in simple houses, designed to keep them safe from the elements. Large, grand buildings, such as the pyramids in Egypt, were constructed for rich people as a symbol of their power. The pyramids also served as tombs for the pharaohs (ancient Egyptian royals). Super-sized religious buildings and worship sites, such as Stonehenge in England, were built for religious ceremonies and as a sign of devotion to the gods.

MATHS TALK

The ancient Egyptians used maths to design the perfect pyramid. In order to make the top of each side meet in the centre, they had to make the slope of each side exactly the same. The Egyptians achieved this by making each angle at the base measure 51.5 degrees. Then, they calculated the angle at the top of each side. If all angles inside a triangle add up to 180 degrees, what should the top angle measure?

?

51.5 degrees

51.5 degrees

The Ziggurat of Ur was built by the Sumerians around 4,200 years ago in the area known today as Iraq. This mud brick temple originally measured over 30 m high, but only the lower levels remain today.

There are no written records of how ancient structures were built. It's hard to imagine how the creators of Stonehenge moved the giant blocks of stone into place without modern machines. Many wonder how the ancient Egyptians built the towering pyramids without cranes to lift the top pieces into place.

THINKING OUTSIDE THE BOX!

Some historians and engineers have come up with theories as to how ancient buildings were constructed. One theory is that the stones that make up Egypt's pyramids were pulled on sledges up flat ramps and then slotted into place. The stones used in Stonehenge may have been transported by rafts and giant sledges and then pulled into place using ropes. Some hands-on historians have even tried out their theories to prove that they are possible!

SCIENCE TALK

Scientists have always suspected that some of the rocks in Stonehenge came from west Wales, which is hundreds of kilometres away from Stonehenge's site location in Wiltshire. They managed to confirm this theory by studying crystals in Stonehenge's rocks, which were identical to rocks only found in west Wales!

GREEKS AND ROMANS

THE ANCIENT GREEKS AND ROMANS WERE SKILLED ARCHITECTS AND ENGINEERS. BOTH CIVILISATIONS HAD ICONIC ARCHITECTURAL STYLES THAT CAN BE SEEN ACROSS THE LANDS THEY ONCE RULED.

GREEK COLUMNS

The key features of Greek architecture were columns with carved details, which were usually placed symmetrically. Greek architects followed specific rules to make sure that all of their buildings looked similar. The three main styles were Doric, Ionic and Corinthian, which can be easily identified by their columns.

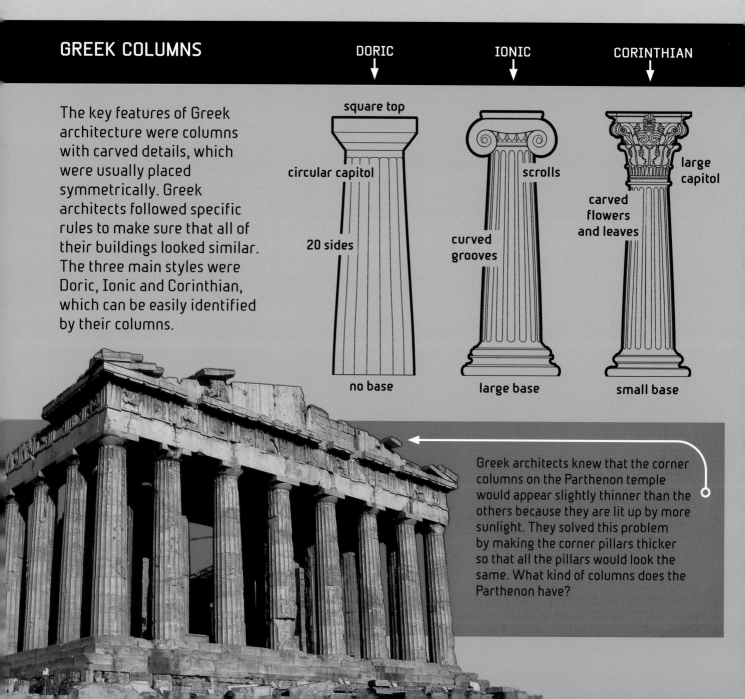

DORIC

IONIC

CORINTHIAN

square top

circular capitol

20 sides

no base

scrolls

curved grooves

large base

large capitol

carved flowers and leaves

small base

Greek architects knew that the corner columns on the Parthenon temple would appear slightly thinner than the others because they are lit up by more sunlight. They solved this problem by making the corner pillars thicker so that all the pillars would look the same. What kind of columns does the Parthenon have?

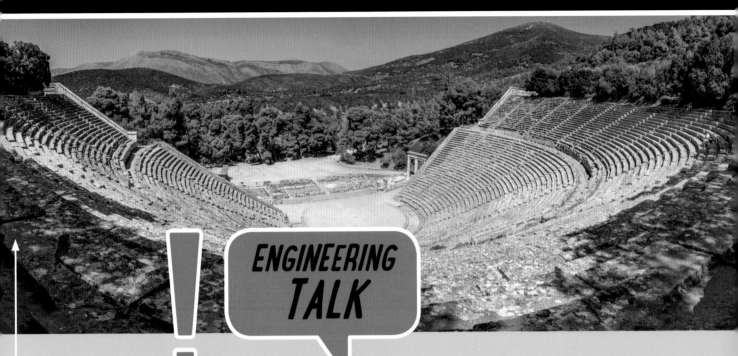

ENGINEERING TALK

As well as looking perfect, Greek buildings were highly functional. The Greeks were huge theatre fans and they studied how sound bounced off different surfaces to give their theatres incredible acoustics. The number one acoustics were in the theatre in Epidavros, which held 15,000 people. Everyone in the theatre, including the people in the back row, could hear something as quiet as paper ripping on stage!

The Romans' development of concrete gave them the freedom to create new types of structure. Instead of relying on columns to support a roof, they could make self-supporting domes and arches from concrete. The insides of buildings could be open and spacious, rather than dotted with tall pillars like Greek buildings.

THINKING OUTSIDE THE BOX!

Concrete wasn't a Roman invention, but the Romans spiced up the recipe by adding volcanic ash. The Romans didn't know that volcanic ash would give the concrete special properties, but as Italy is the only country in Europe with active volcanoes, they had plenty lying around! As it turned out, concrete made with ash did not crack easily and could set underwater – a lucky discovery based on trial and error. Some builders today are considering a return to Roman concrete as it is cheaper and longer-lasting than modern concrete.

CASTLES AND CATHEDRALS

DURING THE MIDDLE AGES (C.5TH-15TH CENTURIES CE), LARGE, GRAND BUILDINGS SPRUNG UP ACROSS EUROPE. ROYALTY AND POWERFUL LORDS HAD TONS OF MONEY TO SPEND AND THEY SPLURGED ON HOMES AND HUGE RELIGIOUS BUILDINGS.

Castles are probably the most iconic buildings of the Middle Ages. They were mainly defensive buildings, built to protect the lord who controlled the surrounding land, but they were also symbols of power and wealth. Castles were designed with features that made them easier to defend, such as thick stone walls, arrow slits, battlements, keep walls and a moat.

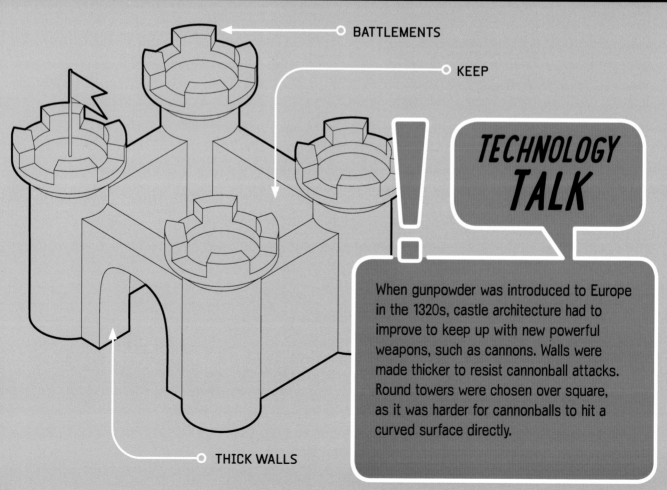

BATTLEMENTS

KEEP

THICK WALLS

TECHNOLOGY TALK

When gunpowder was introduced to Europe in the 1320s, castle architecture had to improve to keep up with new powerful weapons, such as cannons. Walls were made thicker to resist cannonball attacks. Round towers were chosen over square, as it was harder for cannonballs to hit a curved surface directly.

While castle architecture favoured practicality, medieval architects could let their creative juices flow when working on cathedrals. Intricate, elaborate designs were preferred as people wanted to create beautiful buildings as a sign of their devotion to the Christian religion. Medieval builders spent thousands of hours manually carving giant arches and impressive vaults to support high ceilings.

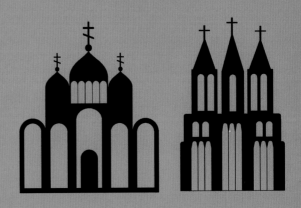

Work began on the Sagrada Família in 1882, but it is still unfinished! It is expected to be completed between 2026 and 2028.

"

ART TALK

Cathedrals and grand churches are still being built today, long after the Middle Ages. Some modern religious buildings are inspired by trends in art. For example, the architect Antoni Gaudí designed the Sagrada Família in Barcelona, Spain, in the art nouveau style, with curved intricate details inspired by nature. The cathedral in Brasília, Brazil, has a modernist, abstract design that was popular in the 1950s and 60s.

"

The cathedral in Brasília has traditional elements of religious buildings, such as stained glass windows, combined with striking modern concrete columns.

THE CREATIVITY AND TECHNICAL SKILLS OF ARCHITECTS ARE TO THANK FOR SOME OF THE MOST ICONIC BUILDINGS IN HISTORY. THESE ARCHITECTS EMBRACED AND EXPERIMENTED WITH THE MATERIALS AND TECHNOLOGY AVAILABLE TO THEM, AND ESTABLISHED ARCHITECTURAL STYLES THAT WERE UNIQUELY THEIRS.

MICHELANGELO (1475–1564)

Although Michelangelo is particularly well known for his sculptures and paintings, he was also a skilled architect. His design for the subtly egg-shaped dome of St Peter's Basilica in Rome, Italy, is a clever feat of engineering, as this shape puts less pressure on the base than a standard half-spherical dome shape.

ANTONI GAUDÍ (1852–1926)

Most of Gaudí's ornate creations are located in or near Barcelona, Spain, his hometown. His buildings were inspired by nature, not just in their decoration, but also in their structure, with columns, arches and roofs designed to mimic natural supporting structures, such as bones and branches.

SIR CHRISTOPHER WREN (1632–1723)

After the Great Fire of London in 1666, there was a huge demand for architects to repair and rebuild the city. Wren was talented and in the right place at the right time. He helped to rebuild St Paul's Cathedral and many churches, leaving his permanent signature on the London skyline.

LOUIS SULLIVAN (1856–1924)

The development of mass-produced steel in the 19th century inspired the US architect Louis Sullivan to use huge steel girders to support the weight of his buildings. Freed from the restrictions of load-bearing walls, Sullivan built higher than ever before, creating the world's first skyscrapers! Sullivan is well known for the saying 'form follows function' – a popular mindset among 20th-century architects who believed that the shape of a building should be dictated by its use, rather than by what looks decorative.

FRANK GEHRY (BORN 1929)

The style of this Canadian architect is sometimes described as 'destructive' as his buildings tend to be fragmented, made up of irregular distorted shapes. His work does not necessarily follow the rule of 'form over function' as many elements of his buildings serve no purpose other than decoration. However, the overall effect is undeniably spectacular!

The Guggenheim Museum in Bilbao, Spain, designed by Frank Gehry.

Zaha Hadid designed the stunning Heydar Aliyev Center in Azerbaijan.

ZAHA HADID (1950–2016)

This Iraqi-born, British architect brought a distinctive futuristic curved style to all of her projects, including the 2012 London Olympics Aquatics Centre. Modern computer software allowed her to work out how to engineer and construct her characteristic gravity-defying buildings.

HOUSES

HOUSES MAY SEEM ORDINARY, BUT THEY ARE SOME OF THE MOST IMPORTANT BUILDINGS ON EARTH. EVERY PERSON IN THE WORLD DESERVES A SHELTER AND A PLACE TO CALL THEIR OWN.

In Europe, Iron Age (c.1200 to 1 BCE) houses were constructed from branches and dried plants.

For most of human history, houses were simple one-storey structures. Holes for windows were cut out of the walls for light and ventilation. They were covered with animal skins or wooden shutters until sheet glass became more readily available around three hundred years ago. It was only in the 20th century that most homes in the western world were fitted with running water, electricity and indoor toilets.

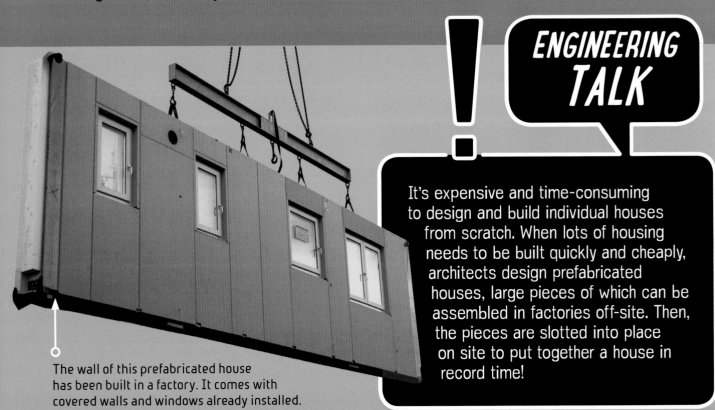

The wall of this prefabricated house has been built in a factory. It comes with covered walls and windows already installed.

ENGINEERING TALK

It's expensive and time-consuming to design and build individual houses from scratch. When lots of housing needs to be built quickly and cheaply, architects design prefabricated houses, large pieces of which can be assembled in factories off-site. Then, the pieces are slotted into place on site to put together a house in record time!

As the world population grows, it has become more difficult to find space to build housing. Building upwards (blocks of flats) is much more space efficient than building outwards (houses). This is why blocks of flats are commonly built in cities, where land is expensive and hard to come by.

MATHS TALK

It's also becoming challenging to find space for housing as the average size of houses worldwide has vastly increased, with people expecting to live in much larger properties. In the past 60 years, the size of a new house in the USA has more than doubled, from 90 m² in 1950 to 222 m² in 2010.

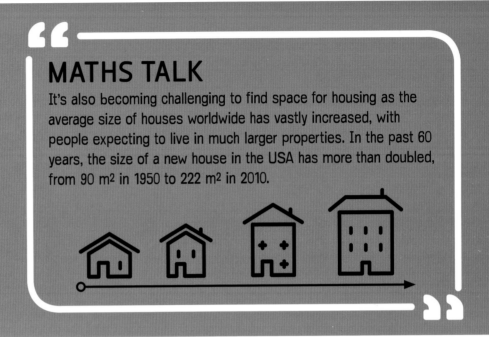

A square metre is a square that measures one metre by one metre. A cubic metre is a cube that measures one metre along each side. Can you work out the size of the bedrooms and wardrobe here in square metres? How big is your bedroom or classroom in square metres?

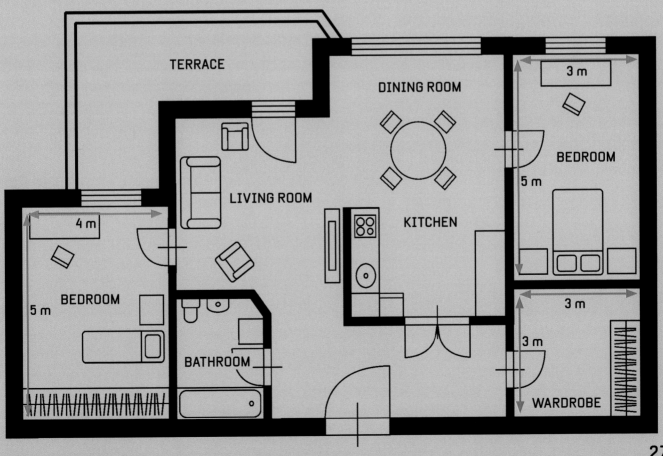

ECO-FRIENDLY BUILDINGS

OUR GROWING WORLD POPULATION IS PUTTING MORE PRESSURE ON RESOURCES, SUCH AS BUILDING MATERIALS AND THE FOSSIL FUELS BURNED TO POWER OUR BUILDINGS. MAKING BUILDINGS MORE ECO-FRIENDLY COULD BE PART OF THE SOLUTION.

Using sustainable materials, such as wood, is a simple way to make construction more eco-friendly. The resources needed to make these materials can be regrown in several years, while rock and metal are non-renewable. Some architects are also designing buildings using recycled materials, such as stone or bricks, from abandoned or damaged buildings. This reduces waste and cuts down on the energy used to create new building materials.

THINKING OUTSIDE THE BOX!

As well as recycling traditional building materials, there are many unconventional materials that can be reused and recycled in new buildings. Plastic bottles and egg cartons, for example, can be used to line walls as insulation.

Old shipping containers can be stacked to create a ready-made building! This block of flats in the Netherlands is made from stacked shipping containers painted in bright colours.

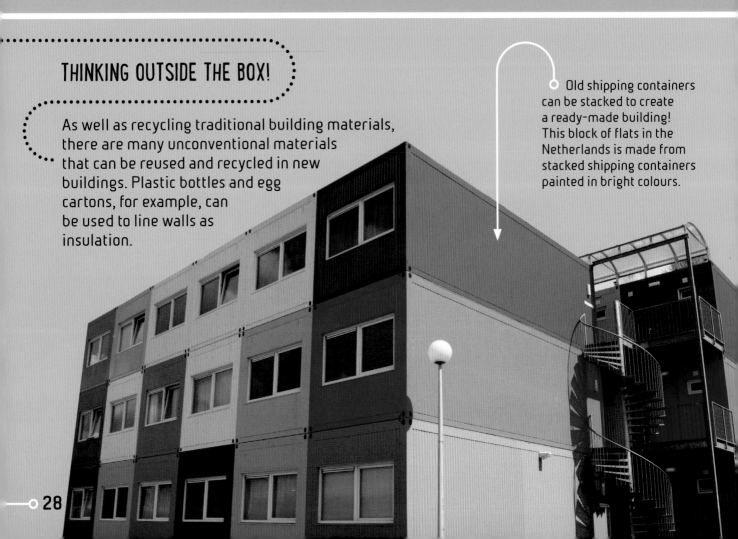

PROJECT

- Test household materials to see if they make good insulators. Place three small plastic cups inside three large, clean yoghurt containers. Pack a different material, such as paper or cotton wool, around the side of each cup in two yoghurt containers. Place nothing in the third container. Put an ice cube in each of the three cups. The container in which the ice takes the longest to melt contains the best insulation material.

- Before you start your test, which material do you think will make the best insulator?

- Why?

- What other materials could you test?

Architects can also make buildings more eco-friendly by designing them to consume fewer resources than traditional buildings. The easiest way to do this is to make buildings as small as possible, while still allowing enough space for them to be functional. This means that less energy will be needed to heat or cool the buildings.

Solar panels and wind turbines are good eco-friendly ways to generate electricity to power a building.

TECHNOLOGY TALK

There are many technological devices that can make buildings more eco-friendly, such as solar panels. Solar panels can be placed on the roof of a building to convert energy from the Sun into energy that can be used to power lights, heating and other electronic items. Some eco-friendly houses also have wind turbines to generate energy, and systems that recycle rain or used water from showers and dishwaters to flush their toilets.

SKYSCRAPERS

CITIES AROUND THE WORLD
ARE FILLED WITH SHINY SKYSCRAPERS
THAT CREATE BEAUTIFUL CITYSCAPES.
THESE TOWERING BUILDINGS STAY
UP IN THE AIR THANKS TO CLEVER
ENGINEERING AND DESIGN.

Many skyscrapers, including the Chrysler Building, sprang up in New York in the 1930s.

As thousands of people flocked to US cities in the second half of the 19th-century, offices and homes were in short supply and land in the city centres became seriously costly. The solution was to build upwards, fitting hundreds of people into one tall, thin building, and the skyscraper was born!

Skyscrapers have popped up in many different countries. This diagram shows the eight tallest buildings in the world, as of 2017. How much taller is the Burj Khalifa than the Shanghai Tower?

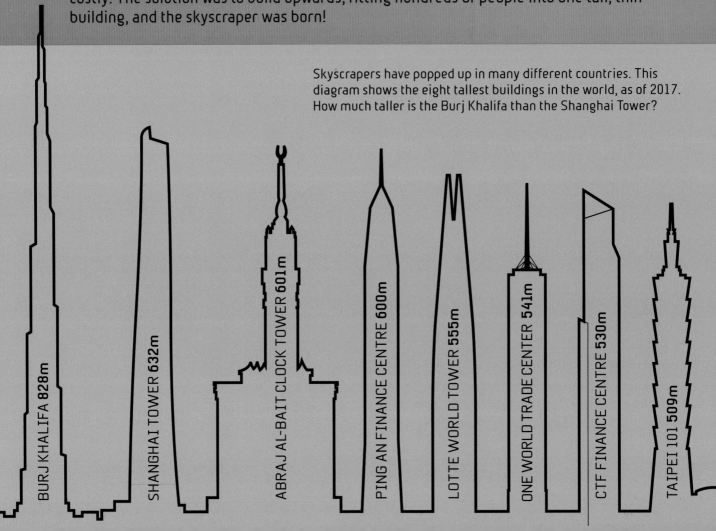

BURJ KHALIFA 828m

SHANGHAI TOWER 632m

ABRAJ AL-BAIT CLOCK TOWER 601m

PING AN FINANCE CENTRE 600m

LOTTE WORLD TOWER 555m

ONE WORLD TRADE CENTER 541m

CTF FINANCE CENTRE 530m

TAIPEI 101 509m

THINKING OUTSIDE THE BOX!

The first skyscrapers had incredibly thick outer walls to support the weight of the top floors, but this took away usable space from the bottom of the building. So, architects added a steel structure at the centre, which supports the weight of the building.

As the outside walls of a skyscraper don't carry any weight, they can be made from glass or thin metal, giving the buildings the iconic shiny look that we know today.

SCIENCE TALK

Designing sky-high structures can be tricky, as every storey adds extra weight. Gravity makes this weight pull down on the base of the building. The weight needs to be balanced so that it doesn't make the building collapse.

PROJECT

- Build your own skyscraper using dry spaghetti and marshmallows. Push the strands of spaghetti into the marshmallows to join pieces together.

- What shape should the base of the skyscraper be?

- How can you stabilise your tower?

- What could you change to make your skyscraper even taller?

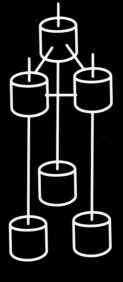

HALL OF FAME: LANDMARKS

THE WORLD'S MOST FAMOUS LANDMARKS ARE OFTEN BUILDINGS, SUCH AS THE TAJ MAHAL, THE EIFFEL TOWER AND THE EMPIRE STATE BUILDING. THESE BUILDINGS WERE CONSTRUCTED AT DIFFERENT TIMES, FROM DIFFERENT MATERIALS AND FOR DIFFERENT REASONS, BUT THEY ARE ALL BELOVED AS ICONIC FEATS OF ENGINEERING AND ARCHITECTURE.

EIFFEL TOWER

The Eiffel Tower in Paris, France, gets its name from its designer, Alexandre Eiffel, who was a skilled bridge engineer. His experience designing bridges strongly influenced his design for the Eiffel Tower, which is made of a lattice of wrought iron, just like many bridges.

HAGIA SOPHIA

The Hagia Sophia was built in Istanbul, Turkey, in the 6th century CE as an Orthodox Christian church. Despite its colossal size and ornate details, it only took six years to build. As a comparison, the construction of Notre-Dame Cathedral in Paris took nearly a century!

LEANING TOWER OF PISA

Most flawed buildings have been demolished or abandoned, but the Leaning Tower of Pisa in Italy is celebrated for its unintentional tilt. Over time, the tilt became more extreme, but the tower has now been stabilised by removing soil from underneath the higher side.

EMPIRE STATE BUILDING

Cheap steel and a desire for more office space in New York, USA, inspired the construction of the Empire State Building in 1930. It stands out from the other skyscrapers in the New York skyline for its height (443 m) and its glamorous Art Deco architecture, with setbacks (stepped sections) exaggerating its height and giving it an elegant tapered shape.

SETBACK

SETBACK

SETBACK

ANGKOR WAT

Angkor Wat in Cambodia is the largest religious monument in the world. Its structure, featuring pointed towers, is designed to represent a sacred Hindu mountain and it is decorated with carved scenes from Hindu mythology.

TAJ MAHAL

The Taj Mahal is a mausoleum (a large, grand tomb) built in the mid 17th century in Agra, northern India. Its simple elegance comes from its perfect symmetry, pure ivory colour and balance of curved domes and straight pillars. It was built in the Mughal style, which combines elements of Indian, Persian and Islamic architecture.

MOST CITIES HAVE LARGE BUILDINGS DESIGNED FOR PUBLIC USE, FROM STADIUMS AND THEATRES TO AIRPORTS AND CAR PARKS. WHEN A BUILDING IS GOING TO BE VISITED BY THOUSANDS OF PEOPLE, IT'S IMPORTANT TO PLAN EXACTLY HOW IT WILL BE USED, AS PROBLEMS COULD QUICKLY GET OUT OF HAND WITH SO MANY VISITORS.

ADOLFO SUÁREZ MADRID-BARAJAS AIRPORT

The main part of this airport in Madrid, Spain, was built in 1927, but its fourth terminal, finished in 2004, is its most exciting feature. Many people find air travel to be stressful, but this terminal is designed specifically to relax travellers before their flight. The architects of Terminal 4 have achieved this by letting in lots of natural light through glass panels along the walls and glass domes in the roof.

NATIONAL STADIUM, SINGAPORE

Rain can spoil even the most thrilling sports match, so the architects of the National Stadium in Singapore have come up with the perfect solution – the world's largest retractable dome roof. Giant panels, weighing thousands of kilograms, can slide together to cover the roof if the clouds turn grey.

PARC DES CÉLESTINS

There's no reason why car parks can't be designed in clever and unusual ways! This underground seven-storey car park in Lyon, France, is built around a hollow central cylinder. A rotating mirror in the centre reflects light through the arches on each level and illuminates all of the building.

SYDNEY OPERA HOUSE

This landmark concert hall in Sydney, Australia, can hold nearly 6,000 guests at once, spread across its six theatres. Its exterior proved to be quite a challenge to construct, as the engineers and architects could not work out a cost-effective way to create the iconic shell shapes. Eventually, they found a solution – making the shells from many arches of different lengths, placed together to create a shape that resembled a section of a sphere.

WORLD TRADE CENTER TRANSPORTATION HUB

This train station in central New York, USA, opened in 2016 to replace the station that was destroyed in the 9/11 terrorist attacks. On street level, there is a dramatic glass-paned structure, known as the Oculus, which lets in light. Inside are several airy open-plan mezzanine levels, with platforms for trains and subways.

BRIDGES

BUILDING BRIDGES IS A COMPLICATED FEAT OF ENGINEERING. DESIGNERS HAVE TO WORK OUT HOW TO MAKE A HEAVY STRUCTURE SPAN A GREAT DISTANCE WITH LITTLE TO NO SUPPORT UNDERNEATH.

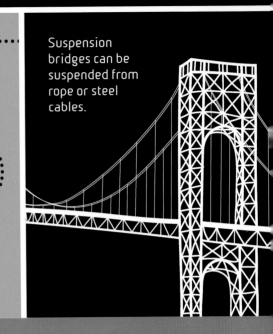

Suspension bridges can be suspended from rope or steel cables.

Early bridges were made from bamboo, stones, ropes, wood and concrete. In the 18th and 19th centuries, metalworking techniques improved and people developed ways of producing large amounts of cast iron and steel. Having access to these materials allowed engineers to design and build much larger bridges with different designs.

The Iron Bridge across the River Severn in England is famous as the world's first arch bridge to be made of cast iron.

Unlike buildings, whose weight is supported by the ground they are built on pushing back against them, bridges generally have nothing underneath them to push back against gravity! If their weight wasn't carefully balanced in other ways, they would come crashing down to the ground. To keep bridges in the air, engineers harness compression (pushing) and tension (pulling) forces to distribute the bridges' weight safely.

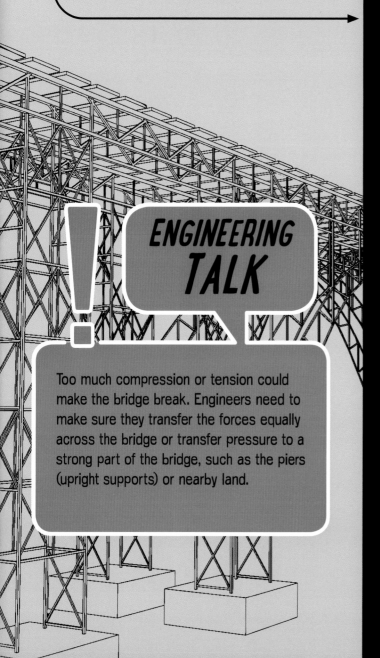

ENGINEERING TALK

Too much compression or tension could make the bridge break. Engineers need to make sure they transfer the forces equally across the bridge or transfer pressure to a strong part of the bridge, such as the piers (upright supports) or nearby land.

TYPES OF BRIDGE

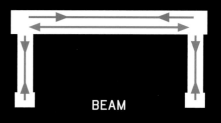

BEAM

ARCH

SUSPENSION

CABLE-STAYED

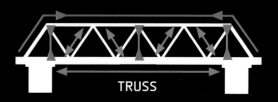

TRUSS

CANTILEVER

■ Tension   ■ Compression

MANY BRIDGES HAVE BECOME FAMOUS LANDMARKS, ATTRACTING TOURISTS WHO MARVEL AT THEIR ARCHITECTURE AND ENGINEERING. THEIR DESIGNS COMBINE ELEMENTS OF DIFFERENT BRIDGE TYPES, DEPENDING ON THEIR FUNCTION, SIZE AND LOCATION.

HANGZHOU BAY BRIDGE

At nearly 36 km in length, the Hangzhou Bay Bridge on the east coast of China is one of the longest bridges in the world. This cable-stayed bridge is so long that it even has a service station in the middle, in case drivers need to take a break!

BROOKLYN BRIDGE

The Brooklyn Bridge in New York, USA, is a combination cable-stayed suspension bridge with a truss thrown in for good measure! Instead of getting divers to work on the piers underwater, the piers were built on top of floating wooden boxes that eventually sunk down to the bottom of the river due to the weight of construction above. The builders then worked inside the wooden boxes to attach the piers to the river bed.

GOLDEN GATE BRIDGE

This suspension bridge in San Francisco, USA, can move from side to side in the wind! This isn't a design flaw, it's actually a deliberate feature to stop it from bending and snapping in the high winds that blow in off the Pacific.

PONT DU GARD

This classic Roman aqueduct and bridge in southern France dates back to the 1st century CE and was built to supply the city of Nîmes with water. The Pont du Gard is made up of over 50,000 tonnes of limestone, cut from a nearby quarry. Some parts of the bridge are made from pieces of limestone that were cut so accurately that no mortar was needed to join them together.

GATESHEAD MILLENNIUM BRIDGE

This bridge in Newcastle, England, is one of only three tilting bridges in the world! The lower part of the bridge can swing up to let boats pass under it, in a movement that looks like an eye winking. The bridge was built off-site and lifted into place in one piece by a floating crane in 2000.

AKASHI KAIKYO BRIDGE

The designers of the Akashi Kaikyo Bridge, the longest suspension bridge in the world, knew they were in for a challenge from the start as its location in the south of Japan often experiences earthquakes and strong sea winds and currents. However, they didn't anticipate an earthquake during construction that moved the towers around 80 cm apart! They drew on their engineering experience to find a solution – making the bridge slightly longer than planned.

TUNNELS

BUILDING A TUNNEL SOUNDS SIMPLE – IT'S JUST AN UNDERGROUND TUBE! HOWEVER, TUNNELS ARE ACTUALLY VERY CHALLENGING TO CONSTRUCT, AS ENGINEERS HAVE TO WORK OUT HOW TO OPPOSE THE FORCES THAT ARE TRYING TO MAKE THE TUNNEL CAVE IN.

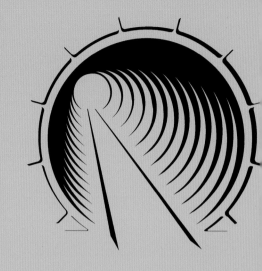

Tunnels have many uses, from carrying water or sewage underground to providing transport routes under congested cities or mountains. The method of constructing a tunnel depends on the material that it is built through. It's much harder to dig through hard rock than soft rock, but tunnels made in soft rock are more likely to collapse.

The Laerdal Tunnel in Norway is the longest road tunnel in the world - it takes over 20 minutes to drive through it. Psychologists suggested that the engineers add brightly coloured lights to keep drivers focused on their surroundings and to stop them from feeling claustrophobic.

THINKING OUTSIDE THE BOX!

Work began on the London Underground, the first subway system in the world, in 1860. At that time, tunnel engineering was quite basic. To create the tunnels for the subway lines, workers used the cut and cover method, which involved digging a trench, building an arch roof over it and then rebuilding the street on top! After the development of the tunnel shield (a temporary structure that supports a tunnel while it is being excavated) in the 1860s, builders were able to work entirely underground and dig much deeper tunnels.

SCIENCE TALK

To balance the pressure of the surrounding rock and soil pushing in, tunnels need to have a strong lining that will push outwards and balance the forces. This prevents the tunnel from caving in. Tunnels are usually lined with stone, iron or concrete, as these materials can withstand strong forces.

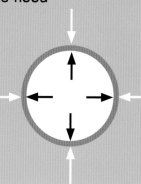

TECHNOLOGY TALK

Builders today dig tunnels using giant drills with rotating circular heads that slice into the rock. The rock and soil that are cut away fall to the back of the machine and are pushed out behind it. The drill can also place supports as it cuts away the rock to stop the tunnel collapsing.

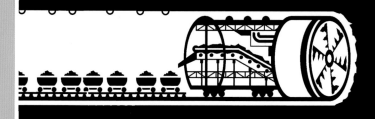

This giant tunnel-cutting drill is creating a tunnel for a new subway line.

WHEN THINGS GO WRONG

TODAY, SOFTWARE CAN PREDICT IF BUILDINGS ARE STRUCTURALLY SOUND BEFORE CONSTRUCTION, BUT THERE IS ALWAYS A RISK THAT SOMETHING MIGHT GO WRONG.

One of the most dramatic engineering failures happened on the Tacoma Narrows Bridge in Washington State, USA, in 1940. During high winds, the cables on the suspension bridge twisted and snapped, making the beam of the bridge buckle. The Tacoma Narrows Bridge eventually collapsed into the river below.

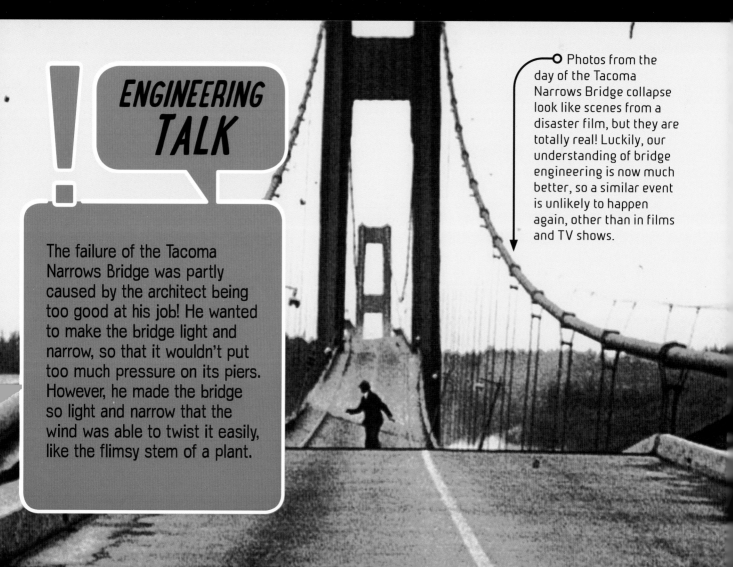

ENGINEERING TALK

The failure of the Tacoma Narrows Bridge was partly caused by the architect being too good at his job! He wanted to make the bridge light and narrow, so that it wouldn't put too much pressure on its piers. However, he made the bridge so light and narrow that the wind was able to twist it easily, like the flimsy stem of a plant.

Photos from the day of the Tacoma Narrows Bridge collapse look like scenes from a disaster film, but they are totally real! Luckily, our understanding of bridge engineering is now much better, so a similar event is unlikely to happen again, other than in films and TV shows.

Some problems are much more easily avoided, as the architects really should have known better. The 'Walkie-Talkie' building in London, England, which was completed in 2014, hit the headlines when it melted a car on the street below! It seems that when the architects decided on a shiny surface for the building, they didn't think about how it would reflect rays of sunlight down to the pavement. The building has since been covered with a non-reflective film.

SCIENCE TALK

The 'Walkie-Talkie' building has a concave shape, which focuses the reflected rays of sunlight into a small area. This makes the sunlight much hotter than typical rays — up to 70 degrees Celsius!

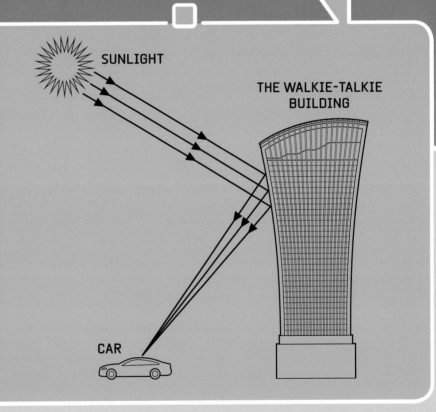

SUNLIGHT

THE WALKIE-TALKIE BUILDING

CAR

THINKING OUTSIDE THE BOX!

Computer programs are mainly used to anticipate and solve structural problems, but they can also help with other details. When architects created a computer model of their design for the new City Hall in London, England, they realised they had problems with sound bouncing around the 500-m-tall open circular staircase. By making changes to the model in the program, the architects worked out how to solve the problem by adapting the stairs to trap sound. This saved them from making expensive, time-consuming repairs after construction was finished.

HOSTILE CONDITIONS

SOME BUILDINGS MUST WITHSTAND EXTREME WEATHER CONDITIONS, SUCH AS WIND AND VERY HIGH AND LOW TEMPERATURES. IN PARTS OF THE WORLD THAT ARE LOCATED ALONG FAULT LINES, BUILDINGS ALSO HAVE TO BE ADAPTED TO DEAL WITH THE INEVITABLE THREAT OF EARTHQUAKES.

Good insulation helps to stop people sweltering in very high temperatures and shivering in freezing weather. However, wind is much harder to control and can pose a serious threat to tall buildings. Tall buildings can sometimes also create wind problems for people at ground level. When wind hits the building and travels down its side, strong gusts of wind are blasted to the building's base.

ENGINEERING TALK

The Burj Khalifa in Dubai is cladded in a heat-resistant material to stop the desert heat radiating through into the building.

All buildings are designed to sway gently in the wind. If a building tries to resist the force of the wind, it is more likely to crack than if it is able to move a little with the wind. However, very strong winds can push buildings over entirely, so architects add strong internal support structures to the centre of buildings in particularly windy areas to resist these large forces.

A popular way to earthquake-proof a building is to isolate the foundations from the rest of the building. This lets the foundations move without moving the building above. The skyscraper Taipei 101 in Taiwan has a giant pendulum inside, which balances the forces by swaying in the opposite direction to the direction the building wants to move in.

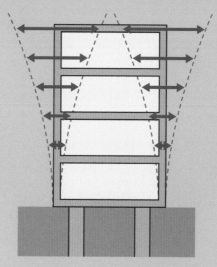

NORMAL FOUNDATIONS

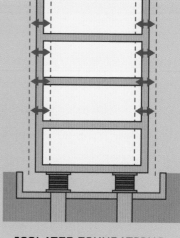

ISOLATED FOUNDATIONS

This diagram shows the difference in movement of a normal building compared to an earthquake-proofed building with isolated foundations.

SCIENCE TALK

Scientists are often inspired by the natural world. In their research to learn how to protect buildings from earthquakes, they are studying mussels to see how they use fibres to attach themselves to rocks underwater. Some of the mussels' fibres are rigid, to keep a tight hold on the rock, while others are flexible so that they don't break in the crashing waves. Scientists believe that a similar approach may help buildings withstand earthquakes.

PROJECT

- Design an earthquake-resistant building using Lego® bricks. Try three different designs and see which is best at resisting when you shake the base.

- How does each building react when you shake the base?

- What strength of shake can each building resist?

- Which shapes of building are better at resisting movement?

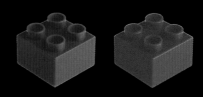

GLOSSARY

abstract a style of art and architecture that takes inspiration from shapes and colours, rather than trying to represent real objects

alloy a metal that is a mixture of two or more metals

aqueduct a structure for carrying water across land

atoms very small particles that everything is made out of

beam a long piece of metal, wood or concrete that supports weight in a structure

buckle to become bent as a result of pressure

compression a force that presses on different sides of an object

fault line the place where there is a break in the Earth's crust and earthquakes can occur

foundations the underground structures that support a building

girder a beam

gravity a force that attracts objects towards each other

horizon the horizontal line at the farthest point you can see, where the sky appears to touch the land or sea

insulate to cover something with a material so that heat or cold cannot pass through it

lattice a structure made from strips that cross over each other

mass how much 'stuff' is in an object

mass-produce to produce a lot of something in a factory

mortar a substance that fixes stones or bricks together when building walls

parallel the distance between two parallel lines never changes and the lines never meet

pendulum a heavy object on a chain that swings from side to side

perspective a way of drawing things so that they appear to be 3D

pier a pillar that supports a bridge

scale the ratio between the size of an object in a drawing and its size in real life

setback the step-shaped part of the outside of a building

sphere a 3D circle

sustainable causing little or no damage to the environment so it can be continued for a long time

tension a stretching force

tessellate to fit together in a repeating pattern with no gaps or overlaps

vanishing point a point in a drawing where parallel lines appear to meet

withstand to be strong enough not to be damaged or broken by something

 FURTHER READING

Awesome Engineering: Bridges Sally Spray (Franklin Watts, 2017)

Buildings, Bridges and Tunnels Jon Richards (Franklin Watts, 2016)

Record-Breaking Buildings Jon Richards and Ed Simkins (Wayland, 2016)

 WEBSITES

FIND OUT MORE ABOUT BUILDINGS AND AMAZING
STRUCTURES AT THE FOLLOWING WEBSITES:

www.dkfindout.com/uk/earth/landmarks-world/

www.pbs.org/wgbh/buildingbig/bridge/

www.sciencekids.co.nz/sciencefacts/engineering/buildings.html

⑦ QUIZ

- What is a geodesic dome?

- In a 1:10 scale, what size does 5 cm on the page represent in real life?

- Name a renewable building material and a non-renewable building material.

- How many years did it take to build the Hagia Sophia?

- Which two main forces must be balanced to keep a bridge safely in the air?

INDEX

QUIZ ANSWERS

- A dome made from triangle-shaped pieces
- 50 cm
- Some renewable materials include wood and clay while non-renewable materials include metal, rock and plastic.
- 6 years
- Compression and tension